HOW TO BECOME A MARKETING EXPERT: THE ONE STEP GUIDE ON BECOMING A MARKETING MOGUL , MAKING PROFITS AND STANDING OUT

James C. Kiely

Preface To Marketing

Marketing is the process of furnishing the proper products, services, or ideas to the proper guests at the proper time, position, and price. It also involves using the proper advertising strategies and labor force to handle any associated client service needs. All marketing strategies are erected on what's known as the" right" principle. We can define marketing as the process of relating the requirements and solicitations of unborn guests(whether they be businesses or consumers) and also meeting or exceeding their prospects by offering products and services. Exchanges are what marketing is each about. When two persons exchange commodity of value in order to meet their individual requirements or wants, there has been an exchange. A consumer generally exchanges plutocrat for a good or service. Some deals involve non-cash exchanges, similar as when a levy for the business charity is given a T- shirt in return for their sweats. One typical misreading is that some people do not distinguish between deals and marketing. Both of these particulars are distinct and are an element of a company's strategy. While marketing is the process of informing guests of the value of a product or service so that it sells, deals is actually dealing the company's goods or services to its guests. Marketers follow the" right" idea to promote exchanges. A implicit consumer will not pay plutocrat for a new camo from Avon if a original Avon salesman does not have the proper camo for them when they need it, at the right price. suppose back to your most recent sale(purchase) What if the cost had increased by 30? What if the store or other supplier was not as fluently reached? Would you have made a purchase? According to the" right" principle, marketers have a lot of influence on the variables that affect selling success. The marketing conception has been enforced by the maturity of successful businesses. The" right" principle is the foundation of the marketing conception. The marketing idea is the use of marketing data to concentrate on consumer requirements and wants in order to design marketing strategies that not only meet client requirements but also achieve organisational pretensions. When an organisation determines the requirements of the client and also creates the products, services, or generalities that will meet those requirements(by clinging to the" right" principle), it's utilising the marketing conception. The marketing gospel is concentrated on furnishing value in order to satisfy guests, whether they're businesses or consumers. The marketing conception specifically entails the following

• Concentrating on customer demands and solicitations to set apart the company's product(s) from those of rivals. Products might be effects, effects to do, or ideas.

• Coordinating all organizational conditioning, including as product and creation, to meet these demands and conditions

• Achieving long- term objects for the company by immorally and fairly meeting customer demands The marketing strategy is presently being used by businesses of all sizes and across all sectors. guests of Enterprise Rent-A-Car discovered they did not want to have to drive to the company's locales. As a result, Enterprise started delivering buses to guests' homes or places of business. Disney discovered that some of its callers abominated standing in ranges. In response, Disney started charging a decoration for FastPass, which enables callers to skip staying in line for lodestones . Knowing that the product is made after request exploration has been conducted to determine the requirements and wants of the guests is a pivotal to understanding the marketing conception. product departments don't only make products, also selling brigades are needed to find ways to vend them grounded on the study. When developing a product, service, or idea, a company that completely understands the marketing conception uses data on implicit guests from the veritably morning, along with other marketing tactics to support it.

CHAPTER ONE

Understanding Marketing Dynamics

Understanding Market Dynamics: A Key Element of Market Analysis

Market dynamics are the forces and variables that affect how a market acts and performs. It entails the investigation and evaluation of a wide range of factors, including supply and demand, rivalry, consumer behaviour, technical developments, and governmental laws. Understanding market dynamics is essential for investors and organisations as it enables them to recognise opportunities, detect dangers, and make well-informed decisions.

Economics and Market Dynamics The supply-supply side theory and demand-side demand are the two main economic theories that influence the supply or demand of an economy.

1. Supply-Side Economics: Also referred to as "Reaganomics," supply-side economics. 'Trickle-down economics' is another name for it. Tax policy, monetary policy, and regulatory policy make up the three pillars of this paradigm. The fundamental tenet of this theory is that the primary factor influencing economic growth is production. The Keynesian approach, on the other hand, assumes that the demand for goods and services may decline. The government can act with fiscal and monetary stimuli as a result of this decline.

2. Demand-side Economics: This approach to economics opposes supply-side economics squarely. This hypothesis contends that the high demand for products and services has a significant impact on economic growth. When there is a significant demand for production services, consumer spending increases and businesses can grow and hire more workers. This has an impact on the increasing employment rate, which further boosts economic expansion. According to demand-side economists, increasing government spending will contribute to economic growth and provide more job possibilities. The 1930s Great Depression is one of the examples they cite. They use it as proof that market growth is more aided by higher government expenditure than by tax cuts.

Why Market Dynamics Occur One of the key inquiries to make is? What factors underlie market dynamics? Market Dynamics are significant variables that affect supply and demand in the market. These elements are a result of individual, corporate, or governmental external or internal stimuli. Human emotions also influence choices, have an effect on the economy, and generate price signals.

1. SUPPLY AND DEMAND is one of the most important elements of market dynamics. The price and quantity of goods or services in a market are determined by the relationship between supply and demand. For example, if the demand for a product increases while the supply remains constant, the price is likely to rise. On the other hand, if supply outpaces demand, the price can go down. Businesses can optimise their production levels, pricing plans, and marketing initiatives by analysing supply and demand trends.

2. Another important aspect of market dynamics is **COMPETITION**. A competitive market has many vendors selling comparable goods or services. Pricing, product differentiation, and market share can all be impacted by the level of competition. For instance, in a market with intense competition, businesses may need to reduce their pricing or provide more value to draw clients. For organizations to successfully position themselves and obtain a competitive edge, they must comprehend the competitive landscape.

3. A key factor in market dynamics is **CONSUMER BEHAVIOUR**. Understanding consumers' tastes, requirements, and buying habits is vital for firms to design products or services that suit their desires. Surveys, market research, and customer feedback can all offer insightful information about consumer behavior. For instance, a business might look at customer opinions and feedback to pinpoint areas that could use improvement or create fresh features that suit customer needs.

4. **A product** is yet another important factor that influences a market. A customer's initial thought will be if the product will be of high quality. A quality product will directly and favorably address an unfulfilled need or desire of the buyer. As a businessperson, your goal should be to use your product to offer value by satisfying a certain need or desire. Ensure simplicity. However, keep in mind that even if you add additional value, a customer who has previously spent a lot of money on an existing product they are dissatisfied with will initially be hesitant to adapt to your product. Before adjusting to yours, they will think about the financial impact, the time and money involved, etc.

Give your product a thorough description to generate enough value to justify the price.

5. Technological advancements also affect the dynamics of the market. Innovations and developments in technology can disrupt existing markets or establish new ones. Businesses must keep up with technology developments and adjust their strategy as necessary. For instance, the creation of online marketplaces and shifting consumer buying preferences are only two ways that the growth of e-commerce has altered the retail sector. Companies can acquire a competitive edge and seize new market possibilities by embracing these technology advancements.

6. Government regulations and policies can have a big impact on how the market works. Market conditions and corporate operations may be impacted by regulations regarding pricing, imports, exports, safety requirements, and environmental sustainability. For instance, more stringent rules about carbon emissions may force businesses to spend money on greener technologies or risk fines. Businesses must comprehend and abide by pertinent legislation in order to operate legally and ethically and to successfully traverse the market.

7. Team : The team you work with is one of the key factors that influence a market. Do you believe that you and your team are capable of competing in the market where you are presently seeking for an opportunity?

Do you possess the information, technical know-how, and resources necessary to succeed in this specific area of opportunity? Never presume that a chance entails achievement. Before entering the market, you should ask yourself these important questions.

● HOW SHOULD I THINK AS A MARKETER?

Why marketing thinking?

• Marketing Allowing means having the guests and their requirements in your mind all the time. • It's a way of defining a proper target request, and preparing a marketing strategy. • Marketing thinking emphasizes the" WHY" of your business.

• Communicating the" WHY" will come an essential part of your marketing plans.

• Your marketing strategy has to explain what you do, why you do it, and why your target request should watch.

• Marketing thinking helps you love what you do, find good guests, and be effective. Do you ask" How to find guests for my products?" numerous companies and freelancers end up trying to find an answer for this question. It seems fully natural. But, let us be fully honest with you " You're formerly on a wrong path!" Why?   Because, if your product comes from the request demand, you know exactly who your guests are, and you have an idea how to reach them.However, that's a clear sign of the product being created at the table, If you ask" how to vend my products services". You might have great ideas, excellent features for your software, stylish design, outstanding quality, low price, but if there's no request for what you have, it's all empty(business wise).   Marketing strategy-

Pushvs. Pull   Creative people can sit at a table and come up with dozens of great ideas for products, services, features or designs. This might be cool from the technology point of view, but it lacks the business aspect. Big companies can go the drive marketing strategy. They produce a product, also they invest millions into advertizing and they simply produce the request for it. Indeed this strategy can fail, if the strategy doesn't produce a request big enough. still, big pots can generally go that. still, the drive strategy is always way too precious for you, If you're a freelancer or a medium- sized company. You simply can not go risking failure. More marketing approach? The pull strategy! The pull marketing strategy means, you fill the request's demand. People or companies have an issue they want to break. You communicate, ask for details, bandy, and only after that you produce a product or a service. You formerly know what your target followership is, and how to reach the implicit guests. You make a network, spread your knowledge and experience. Over time, you make a particular brand. The pull marketing strategy is significantly further effective and less precious than the drive strategy. You can start doing business literally from the ground. structure character, demonstrating knowledge and structure connections take time. Reserve at least one time for it. still, it's worth doing it! Character first, flashing coming Advertising, social media, television advertisements and other ultramodern marketing ways are veritably precious and they do not last. Once you turn your advertisements off, you might be forgotten snappily. Character is what matters! Yes, adverizing will speed it up for you, but it can noway replace **MARKETING THINKING.**

CHAPTER TWO

Understanding Customers Behaviors

You probably have a good understanding of your closest friends' likes and dislikes, shopping habits, brand preferences, and even what they would buy before entering a store.

Wouldn't it be wonderful to also have this level of consumer knowledge? While that objective might sound far-fetched, getting started with a consumer behavior analysis is a terrific idea.

What will be covered in this chapter?

1.What Constitutes Consumer Behaviour?
2.The influences on consumer behavior.
3.Customer Service Affected by Consumer Behaviour.
4.How Do You Conduct A Consumer Behaviour Analysis?
5.Consumer Behaviour Analysis Techniques.

Consumer Behaviour: What Is It?

The term "customer behavior" describes a person's purchasing patterns, including societal trends, recurring patterns, and environmental influences on those decisions. Businesses analyze client behavior to comprehend their target market and develop more alluring offers for their goods and services.

The way your customers shop at your stores, not who they are, is shown by their behaviour. It examines things like product preferences, how frequently people shop, and how they react to your marketing, sales, and service offers. Understanding these specifics enables companies to have enjoyable and effective client interactions.

Customer behavior is influenced by three variables: personal, psychological, and societal. Take a closer look at each type.

Influences on Consumer Behaviour

character traits

A customer's personality, upbringing, and background all have a significant impact on how they behave in your store. Some will be happy and outgoing, some will be calm and collected, and some will be in the middle. To understand client behaviour, it will be essential to know where your target audience falls under this group.

Behavioural Reactions

Because a person's response to a situation is grounded on perception and station, which can alter everyday, cerebral responses can be delicate to read but they've a big impact on client behavior . Consider the following script You lately entered a creation and are enjoying a joyous regale when your garçon unintentionally spills a glass of water on your shirt. Because you are in a good mood and enjoying a nice day, you might be more understanding in this situation. still, you might be more irate with the script if you have lately lost your work.   guests can be patient and happy one day, but   also press your representative about a critical issue the coming. Your platoon may reduce pressure and forestall implicit churn by knowing that a   client's cerebral response isn't a reflection of who they're as a person.

Social Movements

Social trends, similar as peer recommendations, societal norms, or fashions, are outside influences that consumers pay attention to. While some of these factors may have a flash impact on guests, others may have a long-termbon. Let's talk about some data- supported exemplifications of consumer behaviours that have a direct impact on client service now that we have covered some exemplifications of rudiments impacting client behavior.

Consumer Behaviors That Impact Service

The mores in which colorful followership parts like to admit service from the companies they buy from are a awful, practical illustration of how consumer behaviours effect client service. 1,000 consumers were surveyed for the 2022 Consumer Trends Report on the HubSpot Blog to learn further about their preferences and the conditioning they take as a result. We will go over a many of the conclusions below. According to Gen Z, dispatch is preferred for reaching client care, whereas phone calls are preferred by Gen X and millennials. According to your followership base, you should acclimate your client care channels to speak to the preferences of each of your target groups because each generation has a different style. thus, you should make sure that you have further representatives accessible to pick up the phone for troubleshooting than representatives who are watching social media and checking DMs, for case, if you primarily speak to GenX. After outlining consumer behavior and how it affects client service, let's move on to the section below where we'll learn how to assay it.

A customer behavior analysis is what, exactly?

An analysis of client behavior looks at both qualitative and quantitative aspects of how guests engage with your business. client parts are first created into buyer personas grounded on collective interests. After also, keep an eye on each group at the applicable point in the client trip to watch how the colorful personas interact with your business. This study sheds light on the factors affecting your target cult as well as the pretensions, considerations, and strategies used by guests when making opinions. It also enables you to determine whether guests' comprehensions of your business are harmonious with their introductory values.

Why would you want to analyze client behaviour?

Personalization of Content

Customers now more than ever anticipate highly personalized information, making a customer behavior study crucial.

In fact, a Salesforce survey of more than 6,000 consumers found that 66% of respondents expected businesses to understand their needs and expectations, and a Redpoint Global survey found that 82% of respondents expected businesses to accommodate their preferences and meet their expectations. Furthermore, 70% of respondents said they were very likely to only buy from brands that understood them and their needs. In order to ensure client loyalty and retention, you'll make sure to respond to their requirements and desires.

Client Value

The capacity to estimate the whole value of a customer is another crucial business requirement. This procedure is enhanced by a customer behaviour study, which identifies ideal consumer traits. Your company can win over brand-loyal clients before your rivals do by focusing on these characters.

Content Improvement

Your consumer behaviour analysis will yield data that may be used to improve your marketing campaigns. You can engage your most valued consumer segment on their chosen channels in addition to focusing on a smaller group of customers. You may distribute content at the most impactful time by using the results of this analysis.

Additionally, you'll gain knowledge of the areas where each persona encounters obstacles, which will enable you to boost your chances of upselling and cross-selling.

Client Retention

Retaining devoted consumers is just as crucial as attracting new ones. 49% of customers, according to Accenture, expect special treatment when they're a "good customer." These people can start looking elsewhere even if they enjoy your business if you don't have a way to acknowledge them. By detecting both positive and negative customer attributes, a behaviour analysis can assist your team in reducing this customer attrition.

The best way to analyze consumer behavior

1. Create audience segments.

Followership segmentation is the original step in a client behavior analysis. Demographic segmentation(age, gender,etc.), psychographic segmentation(personality,   values,etc.), geographic segmentation(country,   city,etc.), and other factors like behaviors like frequent conduct and product use, preferred media channels, and online buying patterns are important segmentation models.   Also, you should determine which aspects of your guests are most salutary to your company. An RFM study, which shows how   lately and how regularly a consumer has bought from you, is one approach to negotiate this.

2. Define the main advantage for each group.

It is crucial to recognise it because each client persona will have a different rationale for picking your company. Consider the outside influences affecting the customer's purchase in addition to the product or service.

Was it, for instance, a purchase made out of convenience? Or did they consciously decide to look for your company? What is their budget and how urgent was the purchase? A fantastic technique to identify opportunities to enhance the customer experience is to consider the context of the customers' demands.

3. Distribute numerical data.
To guarantee you admit a thorough view of both micro and macro consumer trends, it's vital to

gather information from both internal and external sources. Some coffers can be easier to gain than others.   Your business can gather statistics from within, including information on blog subscriptions, social media trends, and product operation statistics. Secondary channels may give services like competition statistics and consumer reviews. Third- party data offers broad statistics for an entire assiduity rather than being specific to one company. You will have a wide range of data to work with when analysing client behaviours if you combine the three.

4. Evaluate and contrast your quantitative and qualitative findings.

The coming step after gathering your data is to differ the qualitative and quantitative results. Examine your customer trip chart utilising the data sets as a companion to negotiate this. Look at whose persona bought each item, when they did so, and where. Did they pay us a alternate visit? You may acquire a thorough knowledge of your client's trip by comparing the two sets of data against their experience. You should be suitable to spot repeating trends by comparing data. Keep an eye out for typical obstacles that tend to arise at colorful lifecycle stages and make note of any distinctive behaviours unique to a particular client type. pertaining back to your high- value guests, note anything unusual about their purchasing habits.

5. Use a campaign to test out your analysis.

You can use your findings to ameliorate the delivery of your information, as was preliminarily said. Choose the most applicable delivery system for each persona and seize any chances to knitter the consumer experience. By instantly addressing obstacles, you may maintain client connections across the whole client trip. Your consumer behaviour exploration should have given you some useful perceptivity about where to make changes to your marketing enterprise. Use your study to prognosticate what your guests will suppose of the variations before enforcing them. Indeed if a change is for the stylish, some guests will repel it because they're habitual beings. It's pivotal that you keep them as they've a tendency to be more devoted to your brand. suppose of numerous approaches to introducing change to these guests, and keep in mind to be open to their commentary.

6. Examine the findings.

After giving testing enough time, you will really want to know whether your adaptations were successful. Assess the impact of your revised juggernauts with criteria like conversion rate, accession cost, and customer continuance value. Because customer wants are always told by new technology, politics, and events, it's pivotal to continuously assay your issues. By reconsidering your study periodically, you can

make sure you are catching any new client trip
trends.   Do you need   backing doing your
analysis? Look into these tools, which are
excellent for examining consumer behaviour

.

• WHAT MAKES YOU STAND OUT ?

Business requires innovative thinking, and there
are many ways to distinguish out from the
competition with distinctive marketing. Here are
the top 10 suggestions to help you capitalise on
your innovative small business ideas if you're
wondering how to stand out in marketing:

1. Focus

You only have one chance to communicate your message, just like Eminem. The one idea that stands out in their marketing strategy is what they want to communicate to the customer. Avoid overusing language, busy graphics, or several calls to action in your message. Make it punchy, succinct, and brief.

2. Be original

Don't create fliers that look the same as those from every mom and pop store. If you want people to remember and talk about you, try a fresh strategy. Instead of using plain text, use visuals or videos. Instead of using the old-fashioned yellow pages, try social marketing.

3. Exercise good judgement.

Never undervalue the power of well-written content; a catchy slogan or tagline can elevate your message by going viral.

Don't undervalue the harm that poor writing can cause to your reputation either; clients won't trust someone who can't even run a spell check.

4. Looks do matter

When it comes to using photos in your marketing, there are two rules. One: Nothing beats a great image. Make sure the image or design is of the greatest quality and is created professionally. Two: A poor image is always preferable to no image. If you don't have a jaw-dropping image or graphic, don't utilise one that is mediocre or low-res; instead, let your words speak for themselves.

5. Make the most of your headlines

According to studies, you just have three seconds to grab the reader's attention. Use an alluring headline to capture their attention and entice them to continue reading. Instead of listing "5 reasons why our product is great," be unique, detailed, and provide value to your reader by writing about issues that are important to your target audience. The finest small business marketing strategies should improve and simplify the lives of your customers. When drafting your headline, keep that in mind.

6. Honour your unique qualities...

...and support it with data! Promote the features that set your product or service apart and make it superior to the competition, but support your claims with research and concrete statistics rather than empty platitudes ("We're the best!"). For example, "Our deliveries are on time

99.97% of the time - that's 5% more than the next best courier."

7. Maintain a professional appearance.

The days of photocopied fliers and business cards with an email address like mybusiness@hotmail.com are long gone because of the severe competition today.

Nobody will take you seriously if you don't have a professional corporate image and a suitable company email address.

Make sure your marketing message appears as polished and professional as those from the bigger firms to avoid standing out in the wrong manner.

8. Keep up with the times.

Run ahead of the group and leave the tried and true for the crown. What's the newest phrase? Is social marketing going to be big next? Is inbound marketing a topic of conversation? Learn about the most recent trends and start implementing them right away.

9. Appeal to their sentiments

Most advertising fails because it patronises and alienates its target audience by speaking down to them. Be not that person. Facts and precise terminology will help you appeal to your listener's intelligence, which will increase their interest and build their trust.

10. To test and enhance, use data

Your ally is technology. Make the most of the tools that make your website and banners intelligent and adaptive by using A/B testing to determine which layout performs better, scientifically planning your social media posts to obtain the most views, and maximising the use of those technologies.

Use technology to assist you target and improve your efforts rather of taking a general approach. This will help you make each consumer feel valued and catered to.

• WHY SHOULD CLIENTS CHOOSE YOU?

In business, customers may select you for a variety of factors, including their liking for you, their connection with your brand, the fact that you provide the least expensive service, or the best overall value. However, understanding the "why" is essential regardless of what motivates customers to use your services or products.

Understanding "why" a consumer chooses your company over another helps you pinpoint the essence of your unique selling proposition.

So let's look at why people choose you and how you can capitalise on this to expand your brand.

Knowing the why is important.

For your firm to succeed, you must understand why customers choose you. It gives you a chance to stand out from the crowd and emphasize your unique selling proposition.

Knowing why clients choose your company can help you operate the "levers" needed to expand it.

You can target the appropriate demographic with the appropriate message, present the appropriate products and services, expand those products and services, and offer them in the manner that your target market prefers.

Knowing why customers select you also influences your vision and mission, supports the culture of your company, and influences the kind of employees you choose.

How then do you ascertain why clients pick you?

10 FACTORS WHY CLIENTS COULD SELECT YOU

There are many factors, as I just indicated, why a client might pick you, but a few of the more frequent ones are as follows:

THE SOLUTION THAT YOU OFFER

Every company has an issue that it wants to solve, and when you know what that problem is and how it differs from those of your rivals and others in the market, you can clearly explain to customers why they should select you.

You should not just be aware of the issue you resolve; you should also let this guide your company's vision and mission.

It should serve as the cornerstone of your marketing strategy and should be distilled into a concise, memorable message in the form of your USP.

YOU ARE RECOGNISED WELL

Social proof and word-of-mouth advertising can be crucial for business success. A consumer will frequently choose you just because they have heard about what you have to offer from friends or from online reviews.

THEY CAN RECRUIT YOU

Your company needs to be simple to find, both online and offline. Customers frequently choose a company that they can easily Google, learn more about, or that is conveniently located in a place they are familiar with.

YOU SELL AWESOME SERVICES

Brand loyalty is produced via reliable, quality service. Customers will keep choosing you over your rivals when they know they can count on excellent service from you.

THE VALUE OF THE PRICE

The cost of a company's goods or services will influence many customers' decisions, but it doesn't mean the company must be the least expensive.

Customers frequently compare pricing against other aspects of a service or product's worth for their money, such as quality, reputation, and customer service, before choosing it.

THEY BELIEVE YOU.
Because consumers buy from individuals they like, know, and trust, trust is a crucial component of any successful business.

People return to your brand and recommend it to their friends when they believe in you and the goods or services you offer.

IT IS COMFORTABLE
Convenience has served as the foundation for some of the largest companies in the world. A

point of distinction is created if a customer can easily access your goods and services at a time that suits them.

Because time is now one of your customers' most valuable commodities, convenience is crucial.

THEY AGREE WITH YOUR VIEWS.

The development of ethical consumerism in recent years has made customers more concerned than ever with a company's values and ethos.

Customers become loyal when they believe in your brand.

THEY CONNECTION WITH YOUR STORY

Similar to this, buyers frequently choose a company whose story connects with them, therefore it's critical to communicate the meaning and purpose of your brand, as well as its development over time.

THE LAST WORD

Any of the aforementioned factors—although frequently more than one—will influence a customer's choice of you.

They compare your company to the competitors by evaluating factors like as perceived value, service, convenience, beliefs, and a tonne more.

However, it's crucial to comprehend this selecting process and have a general understanding of how they arrived at their final conclusion.

This means that from time to time, you should check in with your client to see how they feel about you and why they choose you.

Knowing why customers pick you allows you to grow and scale your firm while still making it appealing to customers through new products, services, and marketing.

After all, understanding why you appeal to customers and how you may better serve them is crucial to business success. The client is at the centre of each successful business journey.

CHAPTER THREE

Choosing Your marketing Medium

Every organization should abide by the adage "The medium makes the message" when it comes to marketing efforts. The marketing mediums you select for a promotional message are crucial to its success. It's critical to keep in mind that creating the correct marketing mix is more vital than focusing solely on one channel at a time. Fortunately, contemporary technology makes it possible to measure the success rates of a variety of media so that you can determine which media are effective and which require revision.

Every marketing channel, from more conventional ones like newspapers and radio to more contemporary ones like websites and social media, has advantages and disadvantages that must be balanced according to specific conditions. Your message, your audience, and your budget should be your top three considerations when selecting your media. Each of these elements should be taken into account to successfully optimise your promos.

Message

The message is what captures the interest of your audience and demonstrates how they can satisfy their goals and desires. When conveying a message, it must be crystal clear, concise, and reflect the personality of your brand and your target audience. Analysis of the media that will best engage your target audience is required after the message has been produced. For instance, if your company sells clothing, you should reach your target demographic by using more engaging and visible channels like social media.

Audience

Your target customers are your audience. You should build an ideal consumer based on your target market when selecting a medium, and you should research their behaviours to find out which media they are most receptive to or engage with more frequently. You can concentrate on particular outlets that will reach and engage your target audience the most by completing this activity.

Budget

Your ability to choose promotional channels is severely constrained by your budget, so you must be strategic about where you spend your money to maximise your return on investment.

Each medium varies in price; some are quite expensive and best suited to larger budgets, while others are designed for smaller ones. Depending on your target audience and the message you're attempting to spread, any marketing channel can be just as effective as another, regardless of cost.

You should carefully examine your message, your target audience, and your budget when selecting marketing channels. Each of these elements must align with your overall business objective so that you may design efficient and quantifiable promotions to achieve your intended result.

● WHAT MEDIUM WILL BE EFFECTIVE?

Which Marketing Approach Should You Use?
While traditional marketing may be better at reaching a wider audience, digital (online) marketing is typically more affordable and can be more targeted. When choosing which sort of marketing to employ, it's crucial to take your budget and target audience into account.
The finest form of marketing is ultimately the one that best serves your company's needs and objectives.

On a number of platforms, digital marketing is practised. Among them are:

1.Search engine optimisation (SEO)
2.Pay-per-Click (PPC)
3.Mobile advertising
4. Email promotion
5. Social media promotion

1. Search engine optimisation

Paid and unpaid methods are used in search engine marketing to increase visibility on search engine results pages. The e-commerce site will experience greater traffic and earnings as a result of this improved visibility. These processes could consist of content optimisation, keyword insertion, and link building strategies. Paid inclusion, link farming, and content marketing are examples of paid tactics.

2. Click-through marketing

Pay per click is frequently related to sponsored links, pop-up advertising, and banner adverts. The price of this type of marketing is frequently based on how many people click the advertisement or link. PPC marketing is still essential due to its simplicity, high measurable effectiveness, and moderate return on investment (ROI), but as consumers have grown accustomed to seeing ads and links everywhere, the PPC model of marketing has lost some of its significance.

3.Mobile Advertising

The usage of mobile devices like smartphones and tablets is essential to mobile marketing, which is a new type of marketing. Due to application and technology limitations, even though all of the marketing channels previously described can be used to mobile devices, there are important differences that must be discovered and taken into account in a mobile marketing strategy. The rise in consumer use of mobile devices to access marketing content, make online purchases, and engage in other online activities is correlated with the popularity of this type of marketing.

4. Email Promotion

Since the beginning of online marketing, email marketing has been a crucial channel for marketing initiatives. Advertising, newsletters, and other content provided directly to customers who have demonstrated interest in the service or product continue to be incredibly effective methods for attracting people and keeping them as clients. Email conversion rates may be tracked with a high degree of accuracy because to the little window of consumer reactions, which enables marketers to create very complex measurements and plans for this crucial medium.

5.Social Media Marketing,

Large followings on social media platforms like Facebook and Twitter provide firms tremendous marketing opportunities. Marketers can use a wealth of useful information from the ability to assess customer interest in products, companies, and social trends to develop efficient and precisely targeted marketing campaigns. Although using these platforms comes with significant expenditures and difficulties, a highly effective social media marketing campaign can generate a lot of consumer interest.

● WHERE SHOULD I REACH MY CUSTOMERS?

It does not matter how big or small your business is and what type of business it is; mobile marketing can offer you a number of benefits. With the right tool, you will also be able to track your growth.

1.Growing Demand

The entire mobile industry is growing at a rapid rate. Not only that, the growth graph is not ready at all to go horizontal or downward. As a result, more and more people will be able to afford smartphones.

More people having access to mobile phones automatically increases the demand for mobile marketing as it will become one of the most effective ways to reach more audiences.

2..Allows You to Reach a Global Audience

In 2023, billions of people all around the world own a mobile phone. So if your goal is to reach a global audience, mobile marketing is the way to go.Not only can you reach them all, but you can choose exactly who you want to reach. I am sure you have some demographic preferences for your audience, whether it's age,gender, or location.Moreover, ad platforms are getting more sophisticated by the day. Some other popular targeting features include interests, hobbies, past purchase behavior, retargeting, etc.

If you don't know your target audience, you can start broad until you figure it out. Once you determine it, focus on that audience. However, never stop testing and optimizing your mobile marketing campaigns.

3. Multiple Marketing Channels Available

Here's what's great about mobile marketing. There are many different channels and strategies you can utilize to reach consumers.

Mobile Websites

The most obvious one is mobile websites. As I mentioned before, the majority of website traffic comes from smartphones. It is a quick way to check out any website on the go and discover a new brand. The number of purchases made on mobile devices has also been growing. And many predict it will soon surpass desktop purchases.That's why having a mobile-friendly website is crucial.

Mobile Apps

According to App Annie, 92% of Android mobile time is spent in some kind of app. This is another vast marketing opportunity. One option is to display ads within mobile apps. However, you can also create your own app. It can make shopping more convenient, engage customers, and boost brand awareness.

SMS Marketing

SMS marketing is still a widely used form of mobile marketing.

75% of people are fine with receiving text messages after opting in. Text messages have a higher response rate than email or Facebook, and 90% of them are read within a few minutes.

That alone should make you think about creating an SMS strategy for your business.

QR Codes

QR codes are also quite popular when it comes to mobile marketing.Users can scan QR codes that take them to a specific web page with more information.

In-App Mobile Marketing

Ads that show up within mobile apps and games are also very effective and can reach a large number of people. So that's another opportunity to reach huge audiences.Other mobile marketing techniques include email marketing, social media marketing, push notifications, voice, location-based marketing, etc.

4.. Location-Specific Mobile Marketing

Here's one of the biggest benefits of mobile marketing. You can target customers based on location. And that's a massive benefit for any business.

As we mentioned before – people are carrying their smartphones wherever they go. You can take advantage of the geo-targeting abilities of mobile devices. That means sending out location-specific advertisements that are more relevant to the user. You can also use geo-fencing. Geo-fencing triggers notifications, alerts, coupons, or other offers when a device enters a specific location. That's also known as hyperlocal targeting.

You basically set a virtual fence around the location of your business. Or even around your competitors' location (geo-conquesting). A great example of successful location-based marketing is Whole Foods' mobile campaign. It implemented both geo-fencing and geo-conquesting. The result was more traffic to their physical stores as well as their Facebook Page.

5.Cost-effective

When compared to traditional marketing techniques, mobile marketing is significantly cheaper. According to LOCALiQ, ad clicks coming from mobile are 24% cheaper than those coming from the desktop. Optimizing your website for mobile use or sending text messages is less expensive than many traditional marketing techniques.

That's a huge benefit, especially for smaller businesses that don't have a huge marketing budget. So if you want to reach a lot more people for a fraction of the price of traditional advertising, mobile marketing is the way to go. Creating campaign elements is also much easier for mobile. The amount of information you can include in a piece of content is much smaller due to the limited screen size of mobile devices. That makes the content simple, to the point, and thus more effective.

6. Viral Potential

A great thing about mobile content is that it can be easily shared. That also means it has huge viral potential, which is another one of top benefits of mobile marketing. When a user comes across a great piece of content, they will likely share it with their friends or family. Not only does that get you a lot of free exposure, but it can also lead to your marketing campaign going viral, which is not possible with traditional marketing.

7. More Personal

Mobile devices have become an extension of users, who constantly check their phones and keep them close at all times. That's why the information users receive on their mobile devices feels much more personal than on desktops. This is something businesses can use to their advantage. Creating more personal and intimate marketing campaigns can lead to incredible results.

However, to achieve that, you need to make sure you personalize your marketing messages as much as possible.

8. Easy to Track Results

What's great about mobile marketing is that it's easy to track the results of your campaigns. You can analyze responses to your mobile marketing messages and understand the click-through rate. Then, you can simply tweak your campaign to get a higher ROI. This helps businesses be more accurate, relevant, and adaptive.

9. It Helps with Search Engine Rankings

Everyone knows search engine optimization is a complex process. However, one of the things we know for sure is that being present on various social media platforms can help you rank better. If you have active Twitter and Facebook accounts linked to your brand's website, both will appear in search results.

Furthermore, having a responsive website that works great on smartphones is another important ranking factor.

Therefore, mobile marketing mentions can help you boost your SEO rankings. Everything from pay-per-click campaigns to content marketing should have a positive SEO impact.

10. Various Ad Formats to Choose From

When you decide to invest in mobile marketing, there are several ad formats you can use. Generally, choosing the right ad format for your business will help you reach the right audience and get more impressions for the lowest price possible. There are four most frequent mobile ad formats:

- Banner ads

- Interstitial ads

- Native ads

- Video ads

The main benefit of banner ads is how simple and cost-effective they can be. Their success will depend on choosing the right visual, colors, CTA, and ad text.

Native ads are very similar to banner ads, but they are designed to blend better into the mobile environment. Interstitial ads are displayed across the entire screen. They have to be carefully selected because they interfere with the user's mobile experience. For example, if your product is a mobile game, video ads are the best ad format choice. They traditionally have a better CTR thanks to highly engaging visual content. On the other hand, they require some extra budget for video production.

CHAPTER FOUR

Pricing Strategies

Have you ever thought ," That isn't worth the price!" when considering a product? numerous people are willing to spend£ 400 on a incense bottle, indeed though you might not be one of them. This pricing may be respectable to some client parts given the class of the product, the kind of   scents utilised, and the branding.

Marketers therefore use these client hypotheticals and develop price plans in line with them. Although comprehensions might impact pricing, there are numerous other factors as well. The description of price and several pricing objects will be covered in this composition. The numerous pricing options and pricing strategies will next be covered in detail. We will give cases of factual pricing tactics in the real world to help you comprehend these ideas. Pricing can also be characterised as the value consumers abstain in order to acquire and use a commodity or service. In discrepancy to the other factors of the marketing blend, which affect in charges, price is the element of the marketing blend that generates earnings. Because it adds value to the customer, pricing is inversely pivotal as a strategic instrument. The business must suppose about its price objects before choosing a pricing strategy. The company's commercial and overall marketing pretensions should be in line with the pricing objects. The following are a many exemplifications of the numerous price objects

1. bringing in new guests to boost deals,
2. keeping current guests,
3. limiting entry of rivals into the request,
4. limiting request share earnings by rivals,
5. Getting consumers to notice the launch of a new product or brand.
6. Boosting the sales of a certain product range.

• COST-PLUS PRICING

Markup pricing is another name for cost- plus pricing. A destined chance is added to the price of producing one unit of a good(the unit cost) under this pricing strategy. The attendant figure represents the item's selling price. This pricing strategy ignores prices set by rivals and focuses only on unit costs. Due to the fact that it ignores outside influences like competition, it's frequently not the ideal option for numerous enterprises. Cost- plus pricing is constantly used by retailers in the garment, supermarket, and department store diligence. These situations involve a variety of goods being vended, allowing for the operation of colorful luxury rates to colorful goods. Because the value your products deliver is constantly further than the costs to induce the particulars, this pricing fashion is not the topmost fit if you vend software as a service(SaaS). Businesses that want to pursue a cost- leadership strategy should use the cost- plus pricing model. Cost- plus pricing can be incorporated into a business' value proposition by communicating with guests about its pricing strategy and stating commodity along the lines of," We will noway charge further than X for our products." Implicit guests are more likely to trust businesses that are transparent, and this helps them establish a solid brand.

Cost-Plus Formula for Pricing

By combining the costs of materials, labor, and overhead, the cost-plus pricing formula is calculated(1 the luxury quantum). Outflow costs, which are constantly associated with the functional costs of producing a product, are charges that you can not easily link to the costs of accouterments or labor.

Luxury

The luxury is the commensurate difference between the product's selling price and its unit cost. By abating the unit cost from the deals price and dividing the attendant quantum by the unit cost, you may get a product's luxury. The luxury is also calculated by multiplying the final result by 100.   You should examine the benefits and downsides of a cost- plus pricing model before deciding to use it. Then are a many pivotal effects to suppose about.

ADVANTAGES

1. It is easy to use.

A cost-plus pricing technique doesn't require a lot of background investigation. Instead, all you need to do is calculate a markup price by looking at your manufacturing costs (such as labour, materials, and overhead).

2. The cost is acceptable.

Consumers can understand price fluctuations easily thanks to the cost-plus pricing technique. A firm may be able to justify an increase in selling price if, for instance, growing production costs force the company to do so.

It offers a steady rate of return, too.

The cost-plus price should result in full cost coverage when computed properly. The markup % should also guarantee a steady rate of return.

DISADVANTAGES

1. An excessive price can be imposed.

There is a chance that your selling price will be excessively high because this pricing technique disregards competitor prices. If customers decide to work with a less expensive rival, this could lead to a loss of sales.

2. There is no assurance that all expenses will be paid.

Prior to setting the product's price, sales volume is estimated; nevertheless, this projection is occasionally off. Fewer products are sold and the costs to make the product might not be covered if sales are underestimated and the markup is low. The corporation frequently suffers a financial impact as a result of this.

3. There is no motivation to work efficiently.

If the firm bases the selling price, they might still be able to profit from a product at the same percentage even if production expenses increase. This takes away the motivation for the company to run more profitably and pay less to produce its goods. Businesses are unlikely to succeed in the future if they don't change their tactics to reflect the environment.

You can easily add a markup to your product to determine its selling price if you use a cost-plus pricing technique. However, you should consider the advantages and disadvantages of this markup strategy to see if it's a suitable fit for your company.

•VALUE-BASED(GROUNDED)PRICING

Value- grounded pricing is a pricing approach used by companies to set prices for their goods and services grounded on what they suppose their guests would pay. Businesses assess the perceived value to the client rather of determining manufacturing costs and applying a typical luxury, and also charge meetly. Value-grounded pricing is used by social media influencers, automakers, theme premises , and indeed artists to request their goods and services. A many common trueness concerning value- grounded pricing are taken into account by all three of these diligence

1. The price a consumer is willing to pay for a product depends on the request.

2. The value of a product is told by the benefit it offers to the client.

3. Consumers' comprehensions of a product's value might be impacted by challengers' pricing. Companies apply value- grounded pricing after taking into consideration these abecedarian realities, depending on their objects or the situation of their sector. It's applied in several situations, including recognising inelastic demand, which occurs when a product's demand is so great that unit deals would be substantially innocent by a price reduction. largely competitive and price-sensitive requests, where charging further could turn down implicit guests searching for a good deal since the degree of competition generally settles at the price where consumers are prepared to pay. promoting prestige by using advanced-than-normal cheapies to emphasise the oddity and nobility of the product. Dealing accessories

and add- ons to other products that ameliorate their functioning, similar as a relief bowl for your laptop or cell phone if the bone you have is broken. Value- grounded pricing is similar to competition- grounded pricing for cheaper goods, while prestige pricing is relatively analogous to it for more precious goods. Because value- grounded pricing indications in the murky world of deals, consumers must take negotiating into account on a large position. In order for the client to pay a price that represents the value they've placed on the goods and for the dealer to make a decent profit on the deal, consumers and deals representatives should have a discussion to identify the benefits and value that a product provides. The murky world of deals is where value- grounded pricing indications. When using the value- grounded pricing approach, there are a many crucial considerations that every dealer must make. Let's examine three of the most significant bones

.

Scarcity

The value-based pricing approach functions best when used for special, expensive products. Commoditized goods are found in a "sea of same" – a market where options are frequently too fundamentally identical to allow for diverse value evaluations.

Differentiation

This argument is essentially a continuation of the one above: you must be able to justify using a value-based pricing strategy. Most of the time, this begins with you showcasing how you differ noticeably from your rivals.

There must be some form of basis for perceived value. You cannot expect to sell batteries and deliver a product with the fifth longest lifespan while consistently commanding an industry-leading premium.

Prospects typically only pay value-based rates for very useful products, thus producing, identifying, articulating, and projecting genuine value for your offering is necessary if you want to take advantage of this type of strategy.

Segmentation

When putting up a successful value-based marketing plan, market segmentation is a crucial factor to take into account. In general, the model isn't used arbitrarily. Because not everyone is willing to pay value-based rates, you must identify the target audience for your strategy and work out how to best appeal to them.

Several different circumstances frequently involve the use of value-based pricing. Here are a few typical value-based items together with the economic tenets that govern their pricing.

1. Residence

When a product's demand is inelastic, a price reduction would have little to no effect on unit sales. This phenomenon is evident in the housing market.

The American real estate market is predicted to be a "seller's market" in 2022, with purchasers frequently shelling out extra money on top of the asking price for their homes.

A reduced price tends to have little to no effect on the sale of the majority of homes in that type of market. In the face of skyrocketing demand, purchasers make decisions based on how much they think the homes they want to buy are worth.

A few thousand dollars more for a house is it worth it? Sellers have the power to demand higher, value-based prices because even if the answer is "no," there is likely another buyer who is eager to say "yes" to the address.

2. Milk

Markets that are both fiercely competitive and price-sensitive typically settle at the price that customers are prepared to pay. Any higher price could discourage potential customers seeking for a good bargain.

You will observe that milk fits firmly into this group if you enter any supermarket shop. Even though the milk in the cooler may be from various brands, the prices are all within a few cents of one another.

In this instance, the value of the milk is based on the third truth that we previously discussed, which states that consumer perceptions of a product's worth can be influenced by competitors' price.

Hermès Birkin Bag

With higher-than-normal markups that signal the uniqueness and grandeur of the product, brands build prestige. The well-known handcrafted luxury handbag manufacturer Hermès demonstrates how rare its goods are.

Although it's practically hard to purchase one of the bags directly from the maker, they can be found online for thousands of dollars. Buyers place an unusually high value on the bags as a result of the intensive training and workmanship required to make a Birkin bag, which consignment stores like BagHunter take into account when setting their prices.

Swiffer

Selling add-ons and companions to other products can make them more functional.

Sometimes, they are just required in order for the original product to function. Swiffer sweeper mops are a shining illustration of value-based pricing that is solely focused on the advantages that the goods offer to the customer.

A handle and a few sweeper pads are included when you first buy a Swiffer Sweeper. But you'll need to buy more sweeper pads whenever your current supply runs out. When you get at the store and discover that other brands of sweeper pads don't fit your Swiffer Sweeper, the value-based pricing comes into play.

You are forced to buy replacement Swiffer pads directly from the manufacturer because you cannot swap in generic alternatives. Since you had made a commitment to the brand when you purchased the handle, you consequently place a higher value on the Swiffer add-on pads that keep your sweeper in operation.

Five. Diamonds

In the diamond industry, value is largely determined by perception. They are among the most expensive gemstones available, with prices that reflect their exceptional scarcity. In reality, The Knot discovered in 2021 that the typical diamond engagement ring cost about $6,000.

Diamonds are among the most common gems on Earth, significantly more frequent than other stones like rubies, sapphires, and emeralds, despite the perception that they are a valuable resource.

Why then are diamonds so expensive? Simply defined, they are what we believe them to be. Diamonds are a symbol of riches, elegance, and splendour that have permeated all cultures.

The diamond business relies on this idea to inflate the value of the stones and take advantage of value-based pricing, allowing merchants to demand exorbitant prices for jewels that aren't really that unique.

How to Set Your Value-Based Price in 3 Steps

Setting a final selling price with value-based pricing involves a few more procedures. Even though certain pricing techniques, like cost-plus, are rather simple, there are things to keep in mind when determining your final price.

1. Examine your clients

You'll need to be certain of your pricing point because it will only be determined by what your clients are willing to spend.

Contacting current clients who are familiar with your products and services is one step towards achieving this number. You want to find out how much they would pay for your product now that they understand its value. Keep in mind that this price strategy should be largely based on the perceived worth of your clients.

2. Examine all of your addressable markets.

Customer data is important for determining a pricing point, but it's a biassed sample because current consumers have demonstrated their willingness to buy your goods.

Conduct market research to determine the precise cost of obtaining new clients.

To determine how everyone you're trying to sell to values your product and what they would be ready to pay for it, conduct research throughout your whole addressable market.

3. Analyze the competition.

Look to your competitors to examine what they charge and how comparable your product is to what they're offering if your product is fresh to the market and you lack the resources for professional market research.

A excellent indicator of how much your target market appreciates your product is to price your offering similarly to that of the competition. If sales are less than anticipated, it's possible that your rivals' products have greater brand loyalty, which can lead you to use a price strategy based on the level of competition.

Value-Based Pricing's Benefits

1. Market penetration might be simple.

You'll have an easier time gaining market share compared to a diluted or brand-loyal market if your target consumer is not brand loyal or if you are generally unchallenged in your industry.

This is particularly true if your product or service stands out in a significant way.

For instance, luxury goods frequently have great sales when they convey

when they are described as "new" or "limited" and are priced reasonably,

2. There may be higher markups.

The value-based pricing strategy benefits the seller when a product is regarded as prestigious or significant from a cultural standpoint. Buyers in these circumstances don't care how simply how much value customers place on a product, not how much it cost you to make it.

Consider luxury goods like art, high-end clothing, or cars; their markups are quite high since owning these products has additional value. Because of the intangible advantages associated with the product itself, customers are willing to pay extra for the privilege of owning a rare sports vehicle or a painting by a well-known artist.

In other words, your markups can be extremely high if there is enough perceived value:

3. Your perceived worth might rise.

Although value is ultimately a perception that your customers have, you can attempt to change how your value is viewed in a way that is more profitable. Making your goods appear exclusive or renowned through branding and advertising might help you convince consumers that a higher price point is justified.

If including intangible benefits doesn't work, emphasise more of the tangible benefits instead.

actual value that the product generates. For instance, a hammer is only made of metal and

Although carpenters and handymen would struggle to complete their work without wood,

Because of this, the value this straightforward tool produces is enormous.

Value-Based Pricing Drawbacks

1. You might not be using high markups.

Implementing a high markup with a value-based pricing approach will be challenging for businesses that sell commodities. This is due to the fact that buyers in these businesses frequently have a wide range of options. It might be challenging to demonstrate added value in the eyes of the buyer unless your product offers something unique in comparison to competitors.

The wisest course of action is not to rely on value-based pricing in these circumstances because markups may be lower than necessary to develop and grow your business to the required level.

2. It is occasionally unstable.

Perceived value shifts owing to cultural, economic, and technical circumstances that are frequently beyond your control, for better or worse.

If the market grows acclimated to your product and starts to see less value in it, or if a competitor enters the market with a better offering with more perceived value than your product, relying on value-based pricing to increase your contribution margins could backfire. Value-based pricing then requires you to reduce your

prices, which seriously impede sales

3. It's challenging to set your price.

Reaching your value-based price point is less of an exact science, as we've already mentioned. Instead of a fixed markup like you could find in cost-plus pricing, it might be difficult to predict which price point will appeal to every buyer and how a product's worth is viewed across a market.

Although competitor analysis, market research, and customer input might give you some confidence in your pricing point, you won't know the product's perceived value until you put it on the market and compare your sales projections to your actual earnings.

Is Value-Based Pricing the Best Option for Your Company?

Value-based pricing relies on a number of variables, but three are essential to nailing the strategy: assessing how the market influences perceived value, figuring out how much consumers value the goods you sell, and comprehending how your competitors affect your value-based pricing strategy. Although this method of pricing won't be effective for every company, it can be a clever approach to expand into new markets, boost profitability, and improve brand recognition.

Run your sales predictions based on multiple price points for predicted revenue totals to determine whether value-based pricing is appropriate for your company.

●PENETRATION PRICING

More than 17,000 consumers participated in the survey, which found that satisfied customers are 5.1 times more likely to suggest a business and 3.5 times more likely to make another purchase. Therefore, it's crucial to have a solid plan for moving clients up the value ladder after they've made a purchase from you or a clear path to increase profitability - without making your current customers feel pressured to upgrade.

Combine promotions and penetration pricing.

Investigate using a penetration pricing approach in conjunction with special offers, holiday discounts, and the like.

There are three main benefits of providing promotions with discounted prices:

Customers believe they are receiving a great deal and thus link the brand with positive emotions.

This leads to improved profitability as the company only has to deal with reduced margins during the campaign.

No unhappy prospects or customers when prices increase because it is obvious that these reduced rates were only available during the campaign.

Monitor outcomes and modify prices as required.

This is not a situation that can be set and forgotten. To adjust pricing as necessary, it's essential to keep an eye on incoming income, profitability, customer feedback, rival activity, and other things.

In the same way that a basketball player modifies his shot in response to outside factors, pricing must be fine-tuned to guarantee long-term success.

For certain organisations, penetration pricing can be a successful pricing approach, but it could very easily backfire for others. Before putting the strategy into practise, be sure you know how it will impact your business plan if you're interested in using it.

It is crucial to take the time to do it right because price has a direct impact on a company's success.

For certain organizations, penetration pricing can be a successful pricing approach, but it could very easily backfire for others. Before putting the strategy into practise, be sure you know how it will impact your business plan if you're interested in using it.

It is crucial to take the time to do it right because price has a direct impact on a company's success.

CHAPTER FIVE

Making Sales

• CAPTURING LEADS .

How are leads generated?

There are now several forms used to record supereminent information. For illustration, you might use a quotation request form or a lead prisoner form on your website to get callers to subscribe up for your newsletter. You can also use virtual chatbots or pop- up windows to get particular information from callers. Whichever strategy you decide on, it's critical to flash back the following three golden guidelines for lead capture

1. Ascertain the end and purpose of every lead capture peration.
2. Make sure you're offering commodity worthwhile to prospective leads in return for their contact details.
3. Generally, requests for more specific particular information should be replaced with an dispatch address. You have to find the perfect rate of giving to entering.
   Now let's examine a many different styles of generating lead data.

1.The Lead Capture runner

Using a lead capture runner is the simplest system. Eventually, it functions as a wharf runner for specific marketing or advertising juggernauts, offering druggies commodity of value in return for their particular data. Implicit leads are generally directed to this runner via a link from an dispatch, announcement, or search machine results runner(SERP). Information collection is one of the objects of a lead prisoner runner. It must include an charming call to action that convinces callers to give their contact information in exchange for commodity of value if it's to be effective. The right quantum of pay and data sharing must be balanced.

2. Lead Capture Form

Generally, a wharf runner features a form for collecting leads. To gain commodity useful, like access to a webinar or ebook, consumers are anticipated to complete the entire form. The purpose of this is to collect customer data that you can use to increase your conversion rate in the future. It's an excellent way to influence the business that presently exists on your website and cultivate connections with implicit guests. The lead capture form has a minimum of one field where data can be submitted. The most pivotal piece of data you may gain from callers to your website or wharf runner is an dispatch address, which is generally retained for this purpose. You   can   maintain   a   covert communication channel with someone in the future by using their dispatch address. fresh fields,   similar   as   name,   address,   phone number,etc., are also available. But keep in mind that there is a slim chance a prospective lead will supply all the details you need. In this case, the first   print matters more than anything differently. You can always ask for   farther details latterly on.

Give your lead prisoner forms two effects to suppose about   Make sure the offer you are making isstrong.Try not to push too hard to vend. It's your turn to initiate contact in this situation. You can latterly consolidate your relationship.

3. Lead Capture software

Data can be gathered and assembled into a database using lead prisoner software. After that, your marketing platoon can review and use this information for forthcoming systems. Onee-commerce marketing platform that can help you induce leads, convert them to guests, and increase deals is Socital. Socital provides a unique combination of tools for data collection, dispatch database segmentation, conversion optimisation, targeting, and personalization. Another popular choice is Really Simple Systems CRM, a CRM and lead prisoner operation that lets you effectively manage and track each deals occasion throughout the channel.

4. Notes

The final practical tool for effective lead capture is faddish- ups. A pop- up is a graphic stoner interface display area that appears when a stoner is on your website. It generally looks like a little window. Pop- ups have the power to make or break your website. When enforced without a precisely considered strategy, they could be annoying and disruptive. When utilised meetly, they can be a great tool for getting particular data from implicit leads. Leads can be gathered by using pop- ups analogous to the bones below . A click- pop- up window opens when a stoner clicks on any crusade textbook or image on the website. After a website caller has scrolled through a runner and indicated interest in your company, scroll pop- ups appear. After a caller has spent some time on your website, a timed pop- up will display. As soon as a caller lands on your supereminent generation website, the entry pop- up appears. One of the topmost pop- ups for carrying leads is the exit pop- up. Asking" Are you sure you want to leave?"

• **FOSTERING LEADS**

As firms use inbound marketing to generate more leads, the necessity of having a robust lead nurturing plan becomes more and more apparent. Up to 90% of your incoming leads could be lost because, in most cases, only a small percentage of them will be ready to buy straight away. Implementing an effective lead nurturing strategy can have a big impact on revenue, client loyalty, customer retention, and the results of your inbound marketing campaign, among other things.

Actively engaging with your target market by offering relevant information, offering support when required, and keeping a good attitude throughout the buyer's journey is the practise of nurturing leads.

Nurturing leads is critical to the success of your business because these tactics directly impact a consumer's decision to become a paying customer. A few techniques for nurturing leads include personalised content, multi-channel nurturing, multiple touches, timely follow-ups, and targeted material.

Despite all of the benefits that lead nurturing offers, marketers could find it challenging to create a strategy that works around it. According to the 2019 Lead Nurturing & Acceleration Survey, 60% of respondents said their nurture initiatives were ineffective.

Adept marketers (like you) stand a great possibility of outperforming the competition if they implement effective lead nurturing strategies.

Let's move forward now.

Seven Effective Lead Nurturing Techniques

These are the most effective lead nurturing tactics available, regardless of the type of organisation you work for.

1. Utilise pertinent content.

A one-size-fits-all strategy for leading nurture does not exist. According to research, you'll get far greater results if you nurture your leads with pertinent content.

Prioritise understanding each of your unique buyer personas. Next, create a range of content tailored to each of your personas based on their preferences, objectives, aspirations, and marketing triggers.

A marketing automation technology should be in place to help you discover, segment, and target your unique buyer personas as you scale your plan.

2. Implement multi-channel lead nurturing techniques.

Creating a simple email drip campaign and sending generic emails to a list of prospective clients used to be the norm for lead nurturing strategies.

These days, marketers just like you are looking for cutting-edge tactics and resources that go beyond email nurturing. Smart marketers are now using powerful marketing automation technology to support multi-channel lead nurturing strategies.

Effective multi-channel lead nurturing programmes are typically created by combining marketing automation, email marketing, social media, paid retargeting, dynamic website content, and direct sales outreach. Because there are so many techniques involved in this plan, you must ensure that your marketing and sales teams are working together and in sync.

3. Take note of multiple touches.

Even though each product and service has a distinct buyer's journey, studies have revealed that prospects typically encounter ten different marketing messages prior to making a purchase.

As one might anticipate, the best lead nurturing strategies give prospects content that addresses common questions and allays their anxieties as they proceed through the buyer's journey. Think about how you may use a range of content formats—such as social media, blog posts, whitepapers, interactive calculators, and even direct mail—in addition to email techniques to nurture your prospects into clients.

4. Get in touch with leads as soon as you can.

Most companies still take their time to act, despite the apparent benefits of making timely follow-up calls.

Still often, the best method to convert incoming leads into qualified sales prospects is to promptly follow up by phone or email. Using automated lead nurturing, you may connect with large numbers of prospects. This is because following up with a lead immediately following a website conversion greatly boosts the probability of turning that lead into a sales opportunity.

It's far more important to promptly and strategically call an incoming lead.

more fruitful than contacting potential customers by phone. You know exactly what the prospect is looking into based on their recent browsing behaviour. Furthermore, you know enough about the potential client to perform basic background research on the company and role they hold.

5. Compose customised emails.

Because email marketing can be tailored to provide better outcomes, it remains a particularly effective tool for lead nurturing. A lack of personalization caused 41% of customers to switch organisations, according to an Accenture survey. There are several ways that customising emails might support your lead nurturing strategy. You can send triggered emails when a visitor accomplishes a certain task on your website, downloads your gated content, clicks on

links in your emails, or shows a high level of engagement.
When you combine the power of behaviorally triggered emails with marketing personalization, you can send relevant marketing messages to the right people at the right moments.

6. Make use of lead scoring techniques.

For those who may not know, lead scoring is a procedure that is used to Using a scale, prospects are graded based on the perceived value that they individually offer to the business.
Lead scoring may be used with most marketing automation platforms by
displaying numbers next to particular online browsing behaviours, conversion events, or even conversations on social media

The generated score is used to determine which leads need to be nurtured further and which should be followed up with directly by a sales professional.

7. Sync up your sales and marketing strategies.

When marketing and sales collaborate, lead nurturing strategies perform better and increase client retention rates.
Find the exact points in the buyer's journey where prospects should be transferred across teams so that marketing and sales may take turns nurturing leads. Consider a number of triggers, including lead scoring, work flow enrollment, and conversion events, in order to achieve this:

An effective sales and marketing service level agreement (SLA) should outline the shared objectives, responsibilities, and standards for this kind of cross-team collaboration. The two teams will be able to assist one another by creating a SLA.

accountable for creating leads and successfully converting them into paying clients..

Employ Lead Nurturing Techniques

To wrap things off, let's review these seven effective lead nurturing techniques.

1. Targeted content: In order to locate the most qualified leads, create engaging, fascinating, and pleasurable material especially for your target audience.

2. Multi-channel lead nurturing: Engage with and expand your audience on several platforms instead of depending just on email.

3. Multiple touchpoints: Increase the number of touchpoints by employing a range of platforms and content kinds to improve interactions and engagement with members of your target audience.

4. Prompt Follow-Ups: Stay in contact with your prospects to keep them interested and make sure they don't forget about your company.

5. Personalised Emails: If at all possible, tailor your emails to promote customer retention. This also applies to any lead nurturing techniques you may use.

6. Lead score: Use a lead score system to assist you in selecting which leads to prioritise.

7. Sales and Marketing Alignment: Align your sales and marketing teams to improve your lead nurturing tactics and boost customer retention.Any or all of these tactics can help your lead nurturing efforts succeed, so start experimenting with them right away with your team.

• CONVERTING LEADS TO SALES

Lead conversion: what is it?

Converting leads into customers through nurturing strategies including behaviour automation, retargeting, and email nurturing is known as lead conversion, which is a combined marketing and sales process. Lead generation, which aims to convert visitors and prospects into leads, should not be confused with it.

Before a lead becomes a client, it passes through many stages. They begin as a lead, develop into a lead that is qualified for marketing (MQL), and finally become a lead that is qualified for sales (SQL). This implies that marketers need to provide chances for leads to take action towards becoming customers and nurture them throughout the whole lead lifecycle.

Since every business creates a conversion route specifically for its leads, no two are same in their approach. Here are some pointers for developing a lead generating plan for your own company.

How to Create a Process for Converting Leads

1. Compile data regarding leads.

2. Recognise actions with great intention.

3. Align your marketing and sales teams with a SLA.

4. Create the path for converting leads.

1. Compile lead information.
Begin with the information you already have about your leads: their source, industry, firm, number of employees, pain areas, and anything else that will assist you in developing a plan that meets their requirements.

Please remind me to trademark "leads' needs" after I've finished writing it. Now, let's go back to what matters.

"If your conversion strategy is not built around audience data, you will waste a lot of time developing it," explains Marwa Greaves, Director of Global Messaging at HubSpot. "Ask yourself the location of your leads." Are the most interested leads in your newsletter? your online presence? via messaging platforms? Ensure that you are engaging your audience where they are, rather than expecting them to conform to your tactics."

HubSpot's Head of Email and Growth Marketing, Jordan Pritikin, adds one more crucial point to think about.

Recognise the initial reason these leads are visiting your website. "What is the fundamental issue that they are attempting to resolve?" Pritikin queries. "If you can create email nurturing to help them solve that challenge, you're much more likely to connect with them and convert them into a new customer."

If you don't already have the data, try to get it via user research and forms. You may then create a customised conversion procedure from there.

2. In each level, recognise the behaviours with strong intent.

When a lead is prepared to buy, how can you tell? What actions will the lead take? Possessing these responses is essential to distinguishing prospects who are prepared to buy a

a lead who views the price page and your brand's I at the same time as they are ready to buy. Therefore, the sales staff will probably have a significantly tougher time completing a deal if you provide them an unqualified lead.

How would one prevent that? Collaborate with your sales staff to identify the cues that indicate high- and low-intent behaviour. Marketing professionals can choose the appropriate course of action by identifying those behaviours.

3. Align your marketing and sales teams with a SLA.

A lead conversion plan that is not in sync with sales and marketing will be very difficult to implement. You will need to decide on a handoff cadence that is efficient for both sides. A service-level agreement (SLA) can help with that.

Usually, it serves to summarize a contract between a company and a client. To better coordinate their lead conversion strategy, the sales and marketing departments also use it internally.

Each team's objectives, efforts, and accountability metrics for a certain time period, let's say Q1, should be included in an internal SLA. Having said that, this agreement will need to be updated often as the company's goals shift.

4. Create the path for converting leads.

Consider your lead conversion route as a breadcrumb trail that directs potential customers to make a purchase. Offers and calls to action will be incorporated into the journey itself to provide chances for conversion.

Example Lead Conversion Strategy

As an illustration, let's look at the hypothetical UK SaaS startup Zion. The sales and marketing departments at Zion have worked together to create a SLA that consists of the following: Every month, the sales team will get 100 quality leads from marketing, and the sales team will follow up with those leads within a week of receiving them.

Both groups have also put in place a lead scoring system and recognised high-intent behaviors that will set off automated mailings. For example, an email sequence encouraging the lead to schedule a product demo with a sales representative will immediately start when the lead scores 95.

That sales representative will get a message on the back end with details on the lead, their actions, and a schedule for follow-up. The sales representative will automatically send the lead a personalised email if they don't respond within a predetermined amount of time.

This is an illustration of the lead conversion process Zion may provide, both for customers and for sales and marketing on the back end.

Methods for Computing Lead Conversion
It's easy to figure out your lead conversion rate: Divide the total number of conversions by the total number of leads, then multiply the result by 100. The last figure is your LCR.

Example time: Assume you produced 105 qualifying leads between January and February. Twenty of those leads turned into actual sales. This is how the formula will appear: 20/105 x 100. This indicates that the month's lead conversion rate was 19.04%.

Average Rates of Lead Conversion

A single average cannot be used across sectors since lead conversion occurs at several phases and across multiple touchpoints.

A more detailed analysis of conversion rates, such as those broken down by stage (e.g., MQL-to-SQL rate) or channel (e.g., email conversion versus landing page conversion), would be more beneficial for your brand.

Lead Generation Techniques

1. Put behavior automation into practice.

Automation should be used for two reasons: time savings and scalability.

Assume a lead is browsing your website's testimonial section. That can mean that people are considering your goods. Given this, why not programme a follow-up email that might get the lead closer to making a purchase? This can be a product demo or a free trial offer.

Pritikin claims that behavior-based emails outperform other forms of automated emails in terms of performance. Greaves, however, advises marketers to define those behaviors that imply buy readiness from a wider angle.

"Activity-based triggers are an easy win for marketers, but think outside the box when creating them," Greaves advises. "It's not just views on your pricing page that may require an automated follow-up, it could also be views of other customer stories or reviews on your site."

The following is a list of actions that might be automated. In the lead:

• Examine your page with prices.

• Arranges for a product demonstration.

• Requests a free trial.

• Uses email marketing often

• Queries concerning the functionality of the product by email, chatbots, or other means

• Downloads an offer of highly-intent content

To automate follow-ups that convert, it will be crucial to collaborate with your sales staff to identify those critical behaviors.

2. Use email to nurture your leads.

The technique of engaging prospects through email marketing with the ultimate objective of converting them into customers is known as email nurturing. Email lead nurturing requires providing pertinent and useful content.

At this point, the data point starts to matter. You may provide material that interests your leads, fits with their objectives, and overcomes obstacles by using the data you've gathered about them.

To make your emails stand out, consider the following tips:

• Use the lead's name to make your emails more unique.

• Use automation tools to set off events in response to interactions in emails.

• Divide up your mailing list.

3. Make use of social evidence.

Social proof might encourage leads who are thinking about buying your goods or services to make the transaction. client endorsements and reviews, which provide leads with an insight into your brand's client base, are instances of social proof.

When leads are in (or near) the decision-making stage, that's when they work best. As a result, price and landing pages frequently feature them.

You may include user-generated material into your email marketing and social media campaigns as another excellent way to use social proof.

4.Use scoring for leads.

Lead scoring can be useful if your sales and marketing teams aren't able to agree on MQLs and SQLs.

Lead scoring assists marketers in determining a lead's position in the funnel by assigning points to the actions that the lead does. Sales representatives may use it to prioritize leads and determine which steps to follow up on.

Additionally, it guarantees that both teams qualify leads in the same manner.

A lead that meets your sales team's qualification requirements is more likely to become a customer.

5. Use PPC retargeting.

Reaching leads who have previously thought about your brand but weren't quite ready to buy is possible with retargeting. You can reintroduce offers they might be interested in or provide new ones that are more in line with their interests when you retarget them.

Retargeting is a tried-and-true lead generating strategy. Greaves asserts that it can also be effective in converting leads into qualified leads. Brands will need to depend more on first-party data for their retargeting efforts due to the recent limits on cookies, which are frequently used for retargeting advertisements.

Let's discuss some other methods you might increase your lead generation.

Ways to Boost Lead Conversion

1. Begin with analytics or begin with analytics.
2. Describe what high-intent conduct means for your company.
3. Try out different conversion paths.
4. Automate workflows for lead nurturing.

1.Analyse the data first.

Analyzing your analytics should be your first move if your lead conversion rate is low. In particular, your conversion path over a long period of time to ascertain whether the low rate is new or has been steady.

If the latter, determine what could have caused this shift by focusing on the time frame during which the decline began. You might need to try different conversion path tests if it's been consistent.

Greaves advises examining the variations between your conversion CTA positions. Search for the distinction between CTAs that work well and those that don't. Steep drop-offs on specific pages may be a sign of issues with your forms, such as field length, field order, or even the kind of data being asked.

It's possible that marketing overstated what it might offer if the data reveals that leads become less frequent quickly after being turned over to the sales team.

With so many possible reasons, begin with the information provided to guide you. No pun intended.

2. Describe the implications of high-intent behavior for your company.

Many brands might not even be aware that they have problems with lead qualifying. Leads from marketing that aren't prepared for sales interaction may be sent to the sales team, only to be discovered afterwards.

How do you determine which leads are prepared? The first step is to collect accurate data. Speak with your sales staff first to find out what data needs to be gathered. Next, compile an extensive list of behaviors that are high-intent and low-intent so that the marketing team may divide leads into different categories.

This procedure can increase your conversion rate and provide the sales team with more quality leads.

3. Try out different conversion paths.

Consider the lead conversion process as a dwelling. Please bear with me for a moment, even though I know you might be wondering, "Why not go with a road metaphor?" There's always going to be something better in your house, no matter what condition you purchase it in. Items to update, add, repair, and remove. The appearance of your home will also vary as your tastes do.

The same holds true for your route. You can always make improvements to your journey. Furthermore, the objectives, interests, and decision-making processes of your leads could evolve over time and necessitate a fresh strategy.

"A lot of trial and error is needed in lead conversion. If you decide on a plan and stick with it, you won't succeed, according to Greaves. "Creating an experimentation process that allows you to test every part of your flywheel will allow you to learn more about your leads and your own internal process than you would have before."

Even while there's always more work to be done, each trial you conduct will get you one step closer to converting leads.

4. Automate processes for lead nurturing.

Automation is essential when trying to grow your lead nurturing programme. While it might have been effective in the beginning, manually sending customized emails to your prospects will soon become too much to handle as your company expands.

With 25% less time and resources, you can keep the same degree of customisation thanks to automation. After configuring your conversion route, schedule follow-ups to be sent out automatically when leads display specific behaviors.

These strategies might help your team save time while streamlining the conversion process to ensure that no lead is lost in the shuffle. Additionally, this approach frees up time for your sales and marketing staff to concentrate on high-priced goods.

The most important lesson to learn from this is that lead conversion is a continuous process. It necessitates planning, cooperation amongst teams, and a tonne of experimentation.

CHAPTER SIX

Marketing Ethics

The Importance of Brand Transparency in Ethical Marketing
What ethical marketing is, why it matters, and how to become one.

Customers now want businesses to be open and truthful. Customers regarded confidence in product, brand, and business traits as a crucial factor when making a purchase in a 2019 Edelman confidence Barometer Report. Simultaneously, research indicates that brands that are viewed as meaningful or positively impactful have expanded at a rate that is more than twice as fast as other brands.

Companies all over the board are trying to slake the thirst for "social good" as consumers voice their interests and intents by implementing social marketing, corporate social responsibility initiatives, sustainable practises, and other measures that let customers know "we're listening."

However, in a society that values simplicity, does offering a socially aware item or service mean that a business is benefiting both people and the environment? Given that, shouldn't we give our sales process the same moral weight as our products?

It is possible to conduct marketing fundamentals well, morally, and financially. We've developed a set of ethical marketing best practises to aid achieve this.

This chapter will help you rethink your marketing strategies and teach you:
1. What constitutes an ethical marketer
2. The significance of it in today's business

3. Strategies for developing transparent and reliable ethical marketing campaigns

It is possible to conduct marketing fundamentals well, morally, and financially. We've developed a set of ethical marketing best practises to aid achieve this.

This guide will help you reinvent your marketing strategies and teach you:

What it means to market ethically

The significance of it in today's business How to produce open, reliable, and ethical marketing strategies The marketing platoon at Acumen Academy, a network of social entrepreneurs who prioritise successful business over unethical marketing, and Justin Belleme, the author of the B Corp Certified digital marketing agency JB Media, will all be speaking to you. still, first a synopsis

Ethical marketing What's it?

Today's businesses have fresh liabilities. Compared to NGOs, the government, and the media, businesses were set up to be the most secure reality in a recent Edelman Trust Barometer Report. According to the exploration, which conducted checks in 27 countries, pots are now the only organisation seen as both ethical and competent because they've earned confidence by acting as" a guardian of information quality."

We need to define success in marketing more precisely. In order to do ethical marketing, you must give up the short- term thing of month-over-month growth in favour of a long-term growth strategy that focuses on developing connections with implicit consumers, brand sympathizers, and prospects. The following are some traits of moral marketing putting long-term growth ahead of vanity criteria in the near term Managing conflicts to foster formative, candid dialogue within your company putting honesty first yet still understanding the psychology and principles of marketing refusing to give up on the delicate task of determining product- request fit and conveying the benefits of your service or product.

The conception of ethical marketing is that your conduct directly represents who you are. According to Simon Mainwaring, author of We First How Brands and Consumers Use Social Media to make a Better World," If a company has values and the supposition of its actuality is that it's going to play a meaningful part in the world and have a positive impact on people's lives, also that is what you deliver — through your force chain, through your HR department, and the culture you   make through your workers, through the products you take to vend and the way you introduce, through to the types of marketing you do, and eventually to the impact work and community giving that you do."

The practice of doing and speaking morally in a way that's harmonious with your association's values in all areas is known as ethical marketing. As a result, your company's approach to integrating ethical marketing into regular operations will be distinct.

• IMPORTANCE OF MARKETING ETHICS

A recent Forbes research states that more than 90% of millennial consumers prefer to purchase goods from ethical businesses. Furthermore, more than 80 percent of those consumers think that ethical brands outperform other market participants that utilize ethical marketing.

Over time, an organization's total growth and development depends on ethical marketing.

A comprehensive set of rules and standards results in an excellent, well-structured roadmap that is easy for everyone to follow. These are related to definition and operation, therefore they can occasionally overlap with media ethics.

The following justifies the importance of ethical marketing in an organization's operations.

1. Client loyalty

It is among the most important elements of moral marketing. The organization may gain the long-term loyalty, trust, and confidence of its customers by appropriately implementing ethics in business and operations.

Humans have an innate desire to pursue authentic brands, which will undoubtedly yield good results in the short and long term.

2. Extended benefits

The basis of the business or organisation is built on its capacity to prepare for a prosperous future in addition to its ability to endure the present. Brands may engage prospects with high credibility, customer loyalty, a sizable market share, enhanced brand value, greater sales, and higher revenue by using the right marketing ethics. Their right to flawlessly accomplish both short- and long-term goals will be prioritized by these moral actions.

3. Enhanced reliability

An organization gradually becomes closer to becoming recognised in the marketplace and in the eyes of consumers as a true and authentic brand when it strives to fulfill its promises about its goods and services on a regular and consistent basis.

It goes beyond these two examples; an effective process may earn the respect of stakeholders, rivals, investors, and peers, among others.

4. Superior Leadership Capabilities

A corporation that consistently upholds moral principles throughout time progressively establishes itself as a model for other companies to model its strategies and policies related to organisation and operation.

Numerous advantages ultimately result from this, including increased market share, increased sales, respect, reciprocal benefits, and inspiration for others.

5. Exhibiting a vibrant culture

From the outside, this structure presents a pleasant image, but inwardly, it creates a healthy structure and atmosphere within the hierarchy. Higher output results from having a crew that is highly driven and self-assured.

6. Attracting the appropriate personnel to the appropriate location

The firm becomes a lighthouse for well-known people in the association once it can establish brand value in the marketplace.

A wide range of individuals, including potential workers, consultants, vendors, and so on, are eager to connect and collaborate with ethical businesses that really inspire them. This further enabled them to effectively accomplish their aims in a short amount of time.

7. The fulfillment of fundamental human needs and desires

When a business follows the right marketing principles, it may satisfy the fundamental needs and wants of its clients by acting with honesty, integrity, and trust. Long-term exhibition of this has several additional advantages.

8. Achieving financial objectives

The firm needs strong financial partners to support its growth and enable it to achieve major market advances in order for it to continue operating efficiently for extended periods of time. Additionally, it aids in their gaining the moral authority required to attract such individuals.

9. Increasing brand value in the marketplace

When an organization adheres to a suitable code of ethics in marketing, stakeholders, rivals, and other members of the public look up to them. They follow these brands assiduously, giving them enough momentum to make a dent in the market.

● PRINCIPLES OF MARKETING ETHICS

By implementing the following ideas into your daily operations and business procedures, you may gradually increase the level of ethics in your organization and the respect your audience has for you.

1. Make the most of honesty and transparency

Every activity ought to withstand scrutiny. Certain common marketing strategies largely rely on deceit and deception, venturing into a "grey area" that, if one knew all the details, one could call fraudulent. When it comes to marketing, do you adhere to the truth or do you prefer to employ false information and partial truths? Telling the truth to both yourself and other people can assist all parties involved stay out of unpleasant surprises down the road!

2. Put Sustainability First

Strong principles will serve as the foundation for all effective plans and strategies, sparing clients from spending time and money on meaningless endeavours. Make time to do thorough studies of your ideas, the market, and your target audience in order to uncover vital information that will ensure the success, longevity, and ideality of your endeavours.

Businesses who share your commitment to sustainability should be given priority in your marketing and commercial initiatives. This entails closely monitoring their supply chains and other areas to identify and eliminate any unethical behavior.

3. Avoid Using False Advertising

Marketing experts must understand the distinction between promoting a product or service and overstaging it. Exaggerated or incomplete truths used in sensationalised marketing tactics captivate target audiences. In order to attract customers, advertising should emphasise the advantages of products or services and how they will make their lives better.

Most of the time, consumers see advertising with scepticism. Nearly 76% of those surveyed expressed worry over false or misleading information. Furthermore, 65% of respondents think that advertising occasionally provide correct information. Lastly, 13% of people don't believe that commercials are real.

Advertising that is misleading or deceptive should never be used by businesses with strong ethical standards as it can distort the truth and ultimately harm consumers' financial interests.

4. Have Objective Thoughts

It is possible to think and behave morally when you allow your own heart to contribute to the balancing of your thoughts. Our deeds ought to be just since they represent our intentions. Make sure you carefully evaluate your goals to determine whether you are surpassing anything. On paper, your decisions could look good, but they might negatively impact other facets of your life—personal, professional, or those of others. A few little adjustments and clarifications can go a long way towards enabling the harmonious coexistence of the other principles. Still, they exist and will ultimately contribute enough to be noticeable. Sometimes the impacts are difficult to notice or completely understand without experience.

5. Honour customers' privacy

Nowadays, a lot of businesses regularly exchange consumer information, which raises people's concern and causes them to worry more about their privacy. You should feel obliged to take all reasonable precautions to preserve a customer's data and privacy if they provide you with their personal information. Never collect, read, utilise, share, or divulge any personal data on a customer unless you are positive you have their consent.

Reasons for Employing Ethical Marketing by Businesses

Consumers clearly have a sceptical attitude towards the commercials they watch. Ethical marketing can come to the rescue in this situation. It could be effective in winning back potential clients' confidence.

Collaborating with others is crucial to ethical business since it will position businesses as reliable and socially conscious. Nonetheless, businesses that place a high priority on ethical marketing have to view it as an essential part of their objectives and core values rather than as a gimmick. Sustaining advocacy, instruction, and action need sustained work. Businesses that prioritise ethical marketing may improve the world for all.